"THE FABLES OF SAVING"

FUNNY COLORING STORIES FOR LITTLE INVESTORS

FERNANDO FRAGOSO

Introduction

¡Welcome, to a world of fantasy, magical tales of knowledge and financial teachings! I will accompany you on a unique adventure through fables that you will color at your imagination, and that will help you to know the exciting world of finance and money. Have you ever wondered how money works, why it is important to save? Here you will find out. Throughout this book you will learn the adventures of different children, animals and magical characters who will learn very important lessons about, savings, investments, support themselves being generous and responsible.

In each fable of this book, you will discover a treasure of wisdom that will help you understand how money works, and not only that, but will inspire you to make better decisions and create financial habits that will lead to success.

So, take your colors and get ready to color the exciting world of financial fables.

INDEX

The saving rabbit and the golden carrot

One night a rabbit, after having collected carrots decided to keep them in his den. The next day, in the sunlight, the reflection of one of the carrots illuminated his face, surprised, he went to see the carrot and discovered he had a golden carrot. Despite how delicious the golden carrot looked, the rabbit decided to plant the carrot, and eventually, it had a whole garden of huge golden carrots.

The community of saving pigs

Three piggies decided to save money to build their houses, although the three piggies managed to save enough money for each of their houses, each piggy made different decisions. The first little pig decided to buy cheap materials of low quality for his new house, the second little pig decided to use more expensive materials of very good quality, but he hired builders who charged him cheap, but they did not know how to build houses, the third little pig, however, decided to invest all the money he had saved, buying good quality materials, and hiring beavers who are excellent builders. So the three little pigs had their new houses, when one day the evil wolf arrived, destroying the houses of the first two little pigs for not having their houses well-made and with good materials.

The investment turtle and the spending hare

A turtle and a hare participated in a financial race, which consisted of arriving from the lake to the forest taking a photo in each village they crossed. Each photo cost five coins, the turtle and the hare were given a sack with the same amount of coins. When the race began, the fastest hare than the turtle crossed each town with a great advantage over the turtle, so he took the opportunity to buy a lot of food and water, go shopping and partying in each town and take the photo of the race. However, when he reached the last village before reaching the forest, the hare no longer had money to pay for the last photo. When after many hours and at a very slow pace, the turtle arrived, who in each town only bought what needed to eat, drink water and pay for their photos. Continuing into the woods, winning the financial race.

The tree of the dollars

One day, a boy exploring in the woods came across a tree with dollar instead of leaves. The very happy boy cut off all the leaves of the tree causing the tree to wither. The next day, the tree was dry and without any green leaves. Another child walking by discovered the tree dry and withered, the child, decided to take care of it when it began to bloom, was surprised that instead of leaves it had dollars, but unlike the first child the second child carefully harvested the tree, and so the tree continues to bloom with dollar leaves.

The saver kite and the spender kite

Two kites wanted to fly even farther across the sky, so they decided to save to prepare themselves with longer, stronger threads to help them withstand the strong winds. The sparing kite managed to buy a long thread and very resistant, allowing it to fly very high. The kite, which spent all its savings, did not prepare properly and bought a very fragile and short thread, after a few minutes of flying a short distance from the ground, the thread broke and the wasting kite crashed.

The gingerbread house of the merchant

An old merchant, who was too old to continue working, decided to build a gingerbread house, many characters of stories passed by and saw the ginger house marveled, the old merchant decided to rent his gingerbread house to characters of stories. So, the merchant who could no longer work now makes money without having to work and befriends many fairy tale characters who rent their gingerbread house.

The financial marathon runner

A marathon boy decides to start a financial marathon. The child, who knows that running a marathon requires discipline and energy management to reach the goal, decides to save a part of the money he received on his birthdays in his piggy bank, to meet his financial goal, buy the video game he wanted so badly. As in his marathons, he develops discipline to avoid spending his savings and administration to save some of the money he is given. Getting his favorite video game.

The wise owl and the magic coin

An owl received from a magician a magic coin, this coin was doubled every night. The owl who was very wise decided to wait the next morning and took only one coin instead of the two coins, which magically were created. Thus, each day he took only one coin and the rest of the coins doubled night after night, until the wise owl became the wisest and richest owl of all the owls in the forest.

The playful cricket and the saving ant

A cricket and an ant were given money so they could buy toys, the cricket like the ant wanted the new remote-control car that was about to go on sale. However, the cricket desperate for toys went to the toy store and bought all the toys he could. The ant, on the other hand, went to the toy store and bought only a few toys, enough so that when it went on sale the remote-control car could be bought. Now the cricket that has many more toys than the ant, is not happy and sees the happy ant with fewer toys, but with the remote-control car he wanted so much.

The harvest of stars

A space child lives on a dark planet where there is no sun, only slightly illuminated by stars falling from the sky. One day, the boy decided to put all the stars he could into a jar and realized that every jar of stars lit up in the dark. So, he decided to sell bottles of stars, until he could sell so many bottles of stars that he managed to illuminate his entire planet.

The river of the coins

In a magical place near a small village, a river runs, where coins flow instead of water. A child wants to collect the coins but cannot hold them all and loses the coins that keep flowing with the river. The next day, a girl comes up with the clever idea of building a dam and diverts some of the coins from the river to a lake, where they accumulate, so if the river continues to flow, she increases her savings and can take coins when she needs them.

The cat hunter of offers

A very playful cat wants to buy all the toys he likes, but it is not enough with the money he has, this playful cat is also a good hunter, hunter offers, goes to different stores looking for offers for his toys, shop by shop looking for offers, and when you discover the store with the best deal, buy your favorite toys, so you can buy more toys without spending a lot of money.

The balloon of saving

A puppy keeps his money in a saving balloon, which inflates while putting his money in the balloon, the puppy over time became sad because he thought he did not have enough money, however, he continued to fill his saving balloon until one day the saving balloon was so big that it burst, the puppy get very happy because he realized that it had been worth all the time he was saving, and now he has money to buy what he really wants.

Honey of the laborious bees

A bear who was very hungry met a hive of laborious bees and decided to eat all the honey from the hive, the next day he came back for more honey, but the bees no longer had, the surprised bear asked the bees for honey, and the bees told him that he ate the honey that the bees need to eat, now they needed to produce honey for the bees and then for the bear, so now the bear eats some honey every day, and thus allows bees to thrive and continue to produce honey for the bear.

The rainbow of money

A deer reaches the end of the rainbow and finds a pot of gold coins, the deer who is very smart knew that without gold coins the rainbow would go out and could not fill the pot with more gold coins. So he decided to take just a couple of gold coins and let the rainbow keep filling the pot with more coins, instead of taking all the gold coins at once.

The money bridge

A beaver builder decides to build a bridge made of pure coins, but the animals took coins from the bridge and the bridge collapsed, so the beaver taught the other animals that it is important that the bridge has enough coins to make it firm and strong. In this way, the animals learned the importance of taking care of the coins of their great bridge to cross safely from one side to the other.

The garden of the investments

A group of chimpanzees suffered because they did not have much fruit to eat, but a small chimpanzee had the great idea of planting a variety of seeds, the small chimpanzee for a long time, with patience and dedication, took care of the seeds, until they grew into large fruit trees. Now the little chimpanzee has a fruit shop and sells fruits to his chimpanzee friends so that they never suffer more hunger.

The treasure map of knowledge

A group of fish found a treasure map, all the happy fish decided to search for the treasure until they found it. When they finally found out that the treasure was a place full of books and knowledge, the fish waiting for money and wealth were leaving all the books, only a small fish, decided to invest time in learning from the books. Now that fish is the wisest, most successful and richest of all.

The race of the postmen

Two postmen were on a mission to deliver as many letters as possible to earn a reward, one of the most distracted and lazy postmen, saw that the other postman was a novice postman, so he decided to work without effort, wasting time, confident that the new postman wouldn't know how to do the job. The young postman, on the other hand, worked efficiently and consistently. In the end, the young postman correctly delivered more cards, thus winning the reward.

The festival of sharing

A child wants to organize a festival with his friends from the village, but does not have the necessary resources, however, his friends decide to support so each child contributes a part of the resources for the festival, some bring juices, others bring food, others bring toys, and others help decorate. In this way, all the children could enjoy a fun festival without spending so many resources.